The Natural History Museum

Animal Close-Ups

Frogs

and snakes and their relatives

Barbara Taylor

OXFORD
UNIVERSITY PRESS

A 4-8

OXFORD
UNIVERSITY PRESS

Great Clarendon Street, Oxford OX2 6DP

Oxford University Press is a department of the University of Oxford.
It furthers the University's objective of excellence in research, scholarship,
and education by publishing worldwide in

Oxford New York

Athens Auckland Bangkok Bogotá Buenos Aires
Cape Town Chennai Dar es Salaam Delhi Florence Hong Kong Istanbul
Karachi Kolcata Kuala Lumpur Madrid Melbourne Mexico City Mumbai
Nairobi Paris São Paulo Shanghai Singapore Taipei Tokyo Toronto Warsaw

with associated companies in Berlin Ibadan

Oxford is a registered trade mark of Oxford University Press
in the UK and in certain other countries

British Library Cataloguing in Publication Data available

Paperback ISBN 0 19 910788 2

1 3 5 7 9 10 8 6 4 2

Printed in Hong Kong

Contents

About this book

This book takes a close look at amphibians, such as frogs, which have smooth skin, and reptiles, such as snakes, with scaly skins. Reptiles usually live on land. Most amphibians go to the water to mate and lay their eggs.

I am a hopping frog.

I use my long, strong back legs to hop away from my enemies. I live on land and in the water. I breathe through my nose and my cold, wet skin.

I can jump more than six times my own length in one leap.

My toes are webbed, which helps me to swim and move over boggy ground.

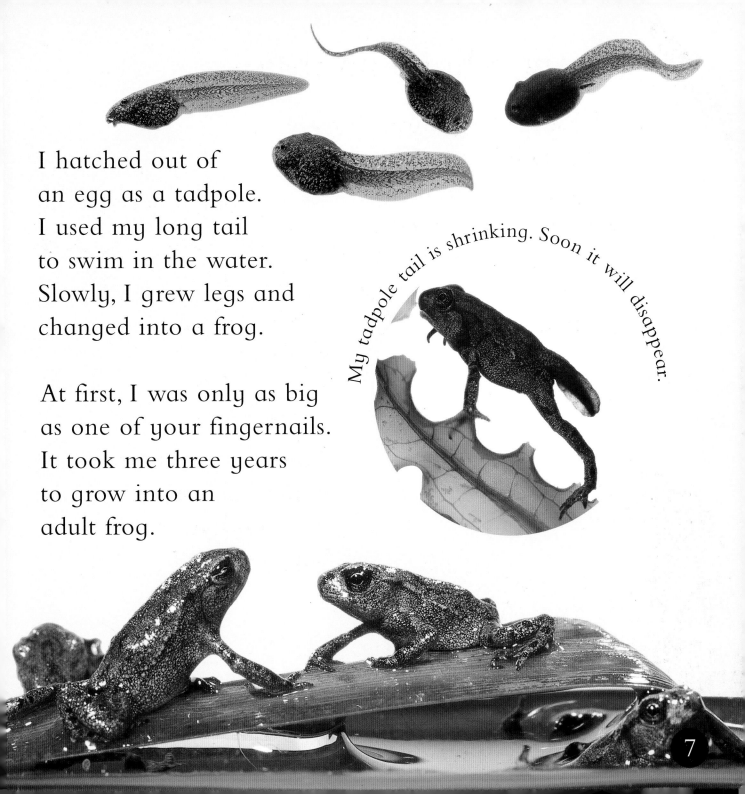

I hatched out of
an egg as a tadpole.
I used my long tail
to swim in the water.
Slowly, I grew legs and
changed into a frog.

At first, I was only as big
as one of your fingernails.
It took me three years
to grow into an
adult frog.

My tadpole tail is shrinking. Soon it will disappear.

I am a warty cane toad.

I live in damp, grassy places. I am bigger than an adult's hand. I can hear well, but I don't have ears like yours. My eardrum is a flat disc next to my eye.

I have lump-like glands full of poison behind my eyes.

I have a huge mouth, but no teeth. So I swallow my food whole. I gobble up insects, worms, frogs and mice. I catch them with my sticky tongue.

My warty skin dries out easily, which is why I live in damp places. My legs are short. I cannot jump and swim as well as a frog.

My bulging eyes help me to keep a sharp look out for prey or danger.

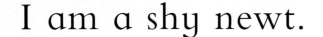

I am a shy newt.

I am called a palmate newt. I live on land some of the time but go back to the water to mate.

I have little specks of colour on my skin.

My smooth skin is not waterproof. I have to live in damp places or I will dry out.

My back feet are webbed. They help me to swim.

I am about as long as an adult's finger.

In spring, I have a thread at the tip of my tail. I use my tail to attract female newts.

11

I am a deadly pit viper.

Beware of me! I'm poisonous and I could kill you. But I usually eat birds and bats. I hunt in the rainforest at night.

I hang by my tail from tree branches.

I have a bag of poison under the skin on each side of my head.

Every part of my body is covered by scales, even my eyes. The scales over my eyes are like see-through bubbles. They are called spectacles.

The holes under my eyes pick up the heat given off by the warm bodies of my prey.

My scaly skin feels dry to touch, not slimy.

13

I am a spotty anaconda.

My spots help me
to hide as I wait in
the water to catch
a meal.

I squeeze my prey
to death in my
strong coils. Then I
swallow it whole.

The big scales on my belly help me to grip the ground.

14

I am a poisonous rattlesnake.

My forked tongue helps me taste
and smell the air. I stare at you
because I cannot blink
or shut my eyes.

My rattle is made of old, hollow scales.

When I shake my
rattle, it means "Keep
away, or I will bite you."
My bite is poisonous.

I am a spiky iguana.

I am a type of lizard. I eat leaves, fruit and flowers. I chop them up with my sharp teeth.

These thickened scales help to protect my skin.

I move my throat flap and my crest to display to other green iguanas.

My long toes and
claws help me
to climb trees.

I can use my long tail to
strike my enemies. My
green colour helps me
hide from them in
the leaves.

17

I am a gliding gecko.

I have flaps of wrinkly skin along the sides of my body. I spread these out like a parachute when I glide from tree to tree.

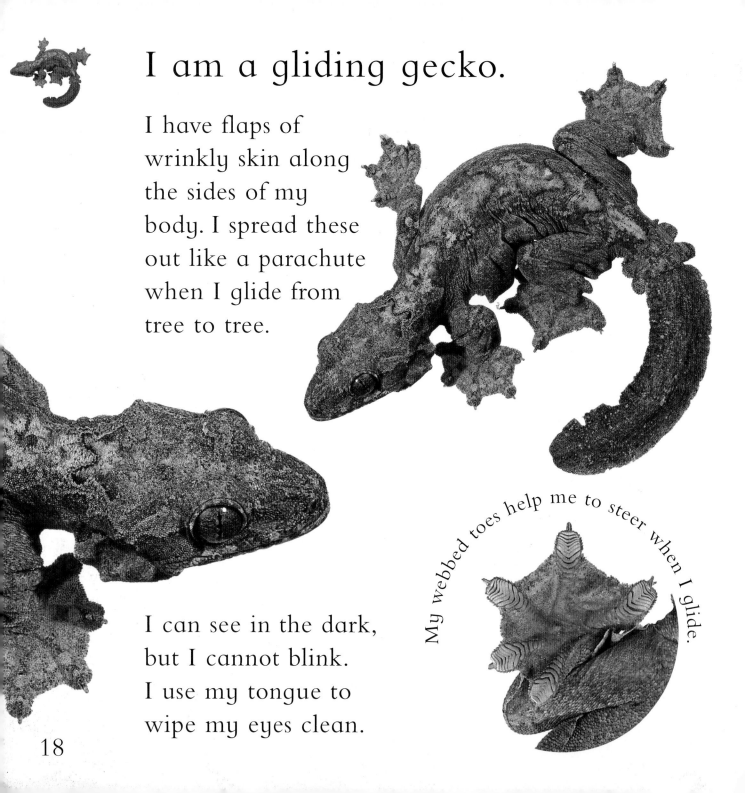

I can see in the dark, but I cannot blink. I use my tongue to wipe my eyes clean.

My webbed toes help me to steer when I glide.

18

I am a slow turtle.

My hard shell is like a
suit of armour. It protects
me from enemies. I live
in ponds and rice fields
in China.

My sharp claws help me to grip wet, slippery surfaces.

I have a top shell and a bottom shell.

I can pull my
head right
inside my shell.

I am a scaly caiman.

I am like an alligator,
but smaller. I live in rivers,
lakes and swamps.

My beady eyes can even see in the dark.

I snap up fish with my strong jaws and spiky teeth.

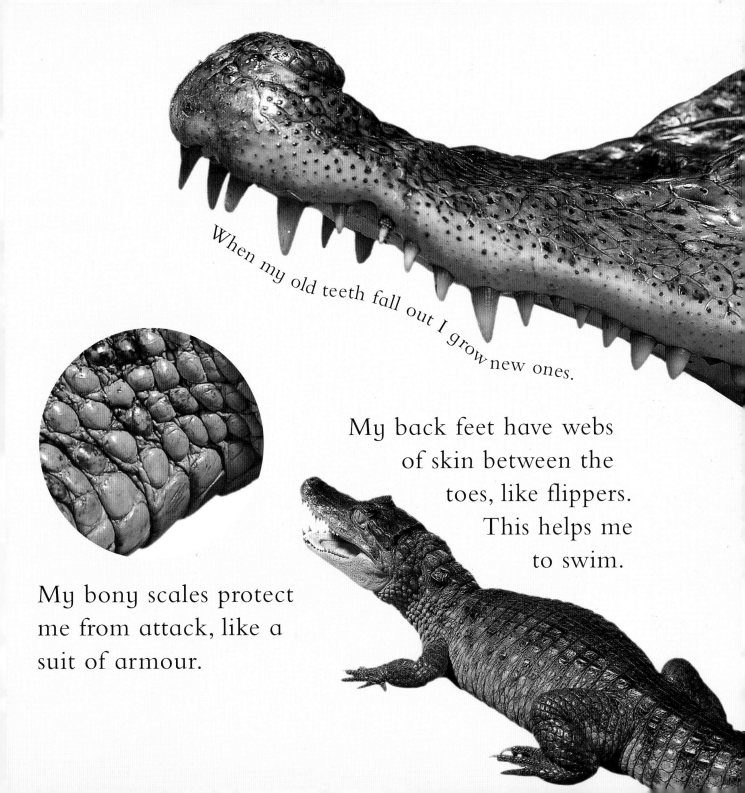

When my old teeth fall out I grow new ones.

My back feet have webs of skin between the toes, like flippers. This helps me to swim.

My bony scales protect me from attack, like a suit of armour.

Important words

display Showing off parts of the body, to attract a mate.

lizard A reptile that usually has four legs, sharp claws and a long tail.

mate One of a pair of animals that come together to produce young.

prey An animal that is killed or eaten by another animal.

scales Thin, hard, overlapping plates that protect the skin of fishes and reptiles.

viper A very poisonous snake with a short thick body and a wide head.

Index